Contents

T0204234

the Community College Story

SECOND EDITION

George B. Vaughan

COMMUNITY COLLEGE PRESS®
a division of the American Association
of Community Colleges, Washington, D.C.

The American Association of Community Colleges (AACC) is the primary advocacy organization for the nation's community colleges. The association represents 1,100 two-year, associate degree-granting institutions and some 10 million students. AACC provides leadership and service in five key areas: policy initiatives, advocacy, research, education services, and coordination/networking.

Requests for permission should be sent to

Community College Press
American Association of Community Colleges
One Dupont Circle, NW
Suite 410
Washington, DC 20036
Fax: (202) 223-9390

Printed in the United States of America.

ISBN 0-87117-323-9

Figures _____

*Tables*_____

Foreword

Community colleges have served the nation for a century, and they continue to respond to community needs with innovative strategies for learning. *The Community College Story*, commissioned by the American Association of Community Colleges (AACC), offers a brief overview of the rich history and important role of community colleges in the United States and describes some of the political and societal influences that prompted their development.

This work touches on important themes related to the community college mission, including open access and equity, comprehensive services, meeting community needs, and commitment to teaching and lifelong learning. It looks at the various programs and curricula common to community colleges. The work offers a brief profile of the community college student and faculty and an overview of funding sources and governance. It includes highlights in community college history and a look at the future.

In this second edition of *The Community College Story*, the statistical information, time line, and reading list have been updated, and a list of Internet resources has been added. The text has been revised to take into account the ever-evolving characteristics of community colleges and the students and communities they serve.

Many thanks to George Vaughan for his contribution to the understanding of events and themes surrounding the community college during its first century of innovation.

David R. Pierce
President Emeritus
American Association of Community Colleges

1 ◆ *The Community College* _____

T he American community college has strong roots in the nation's history and its commitment to expanding educational opportunity for all. Borrowing from the public high school, the private junior college, and the four-year college and university, the community college combined characteristics of all these institutions but has developed its own identity. Influenced by such diverse forces as the rapid expansion of the public high school after 1890, calls for the reform of American education by university leaders and scholars early in the 20th century, the GI Bill, the baby boom, business and industry's demand for trained workers, the civil rights movement of the 1960s, federal student aid, and thousands of state legislators and laws, today's community college embodies Thomas Jefferson's belief that education should be practical as well as liberal and should serve the public good as well as individual needs.

Many people never would have attended college were it not for community colleges and their commitment to open-access admissions.

There are about 1,100 community colleges, technical colleges, two-year branch colleges, tribal colleges, and independent junior colleges in the United States. Of these, about 970 are public institutions. The public colleges serve about 10 million students per year—five million in credit courses and another five million in noncredit courses, activities, and programs. About 45 percent of all first-time college students and 49 percent of all minority college students attend a community college. About 51 percent of community college students are first-generation students—neither parent attended college. Many people never would have attended college were it not for community

TABLE 1.1

Number of Community Colleges by Control of Institution: 1900 to 1998

Year	Public & Tribal	Independent	Total
1900	0	8	8
1915	19	55	74
1920	70	137	207
1925	136	189	325
1930	178	258	436
1935	223	309	532
1940	258	317	575
1945	261	323	584
1950	337	311	648
1955	338	260	598
1960	390	273	663
1965	503	268	771
1970	847	244	1,091
1975	1,014	216	1,230
1980	1,049	182	1,231
1985	1,068	154	1,222
1990	1,282	183	1,465
1995	975	168	1,143
1998	995	137	1,132

Source: National Center for Education Statistics and American Association of Community Colleges

TABLE 1.2

Fall Headcount Enrollment by Type of Institution: 1975 to 1997

Year	Community Colleges	Four-Year Colleges
1975	3,970,119	7,214,740
1980	4,526,287	7,570,608
1985	4,531,077	7,715,978
1990	5,240,083	8,578,554
1995	5,492,529	8,769,252
1997	5,497,420	8,802,835

Source: National Center for Education Statistics

colleges and their commitment to open-access admissions. In addition to offering credit and noncredit courses to a broad constituency, many community colleges serve as cultural, social, and intellectual hubs in their communities.

For the purposes of this discussion, a community college is defined as a regionally accredited institution of higher education that offers the associate degree as its highest degree. Most community colleges are public and receive financial support from public tax dollars. Community colleges primarily serve commuter students, and most community colleges do not have residential facilities.

Every community college has its own culture and serves a unique geographic area and clientele.

Every community college has its own culture and serves a unique geographic area and clientele. Nevertheless, they also share many of the same values, goals, and ideals for themselves and their students. Community colleges are distinguished from other institutions of higher education by their commitment to the values of open access and community building. These fundamental values do much to shape the role and scope of community colleges.

2 ◆ *The Mission* _____

T he community college mission is the fountain from which all of its activities flow. In a few words, this mission is to provide access to postsecondary educational programs and services that lead to stronger, more vital communities. The way individual community colleges achieve this mission may differ considerably. Some colleges emphasize college transfer programs; others emphasize technical education. The mission of offering courses, programs, training, and other educational services, however, is essentially the same for all community colleges. The mission of most community colleges is shaped by these commitments:

- Serving all segments of society through an open-access admissions policy that offers equal and fair treatment to all students.
- Providing a comprehensive educational program.
- Serving the community as a community-based institution of higher education.
- Teaching and learning.
- Fostering lifelong learning.

Open Access and Equity

Access has been a major theme in higher education since the end of World War II, and community colleges have been at the center of the promotion of universal higher education. These two-year colleges have not always been open-access institutions, however. Three events contributed to making them so.

First, the children born to returning veterans of World War II—the baby boomers—reached college age during the 1960s. Along with their parents, many of whom attended college with the help of the GI Bill, the baby boomers came to realize that their future opportunities would be closely linked to a college education.

Second, the civil rights movement and the push for women's rights broke down some of the barriers to disadvantaged groups. Eliminating poverty and ignorance became important national goals of the Great Society envisioned by President Lyndon B. Johnson and other national leaders, who promoted education, including higher

Community colleges' commitment to open access in their admissions policies is perhaps the most misunderstood concept associated with these colleges.

education, as the most important means for achieving these goals.

Third, the demands for political and social action during the 1960s and early 1970s resulted in a federal commitment to increase financial aid for higher education. The Higher Education Act of 1965 and subsequent legislation at the national level made it possible for virtually anyone who could establish the need to receive financial assistance to attend college. The Higher Education Act, along with other federal and state programs, continues to provide financial assistance to students who need it.

Open access to higher education, as practiced by the community college, is a manifestation of the belief that a democracy can thrive, indeed survive, only if its people are educated to their fullest potential. Basic to the community college mission, then, is a commitment to open access in its admissions policies and to fair and equal treatment of all students. Access is achieved by maintaining a low tuition rate and offering program choices; equity by removing artificial barriers to access for those traditionally unserved by higher education.

Access and equity mean more than just open admissions. They mean having a college within commuting distance of most residents and giving students choices in what they study. Open access and equity mean that once a student is enrolled, the college provides support services, including counseling, academic advising, and financial aid, helping to ensure that every student has the opportunity to succeed academically. Many colleges offer childcare, flexible scheduling, and distance education as part of their efforts to serve a population with diverse needs. Open access and equity mean that men and women from all ethnic and economic backgrounds can afford to attend the community college and no one is discriminated against in any academic program or service offered by the college.

Community colleges' commitment to open access in their admissions policies is perhaps the most misunderstood concept associated with these colleges. Open access does not mean that anyone can enter any program without the competencies required for effective learning. The prerequisites for entering the college transfer program at a community college are no different than they are at most four-year colleges and universities. The same is true of students entering any number of professional programs, such as nursing. Nevertheless, the community college differs from many institutions in the nation and in the world in the following way: Rather than turn away people who do not have the prerequisites for college-level work, the community college offers avenues for students to obtain the necessary prerequisites.

The Key

One way to illustrate the community college's commitment to access is to imagine each student having a key that represents educational achievement.

A student who approaches a community college will find the main door open and therefore will not need the key to enter. A student who ultimately wishes to earn a bachelor's degree, however, will look for the door labeled College Transfer, which does require a key in the form of prerequisites such as college-preparatory mathematics.

If the student's key will not open the College Transfer door, there are alternatives, such as short-term training leading to immediate employment, for which the student's key may be ready. Or the student can find the door labeled Developmental and Pre-College Courses. Like the door to the college, this one is open and does not require a key. Upon completion of developmental courses, the student may find it possible to open the door to College Transfer and continue on the path to a degree.

Access does not mean anyone can enter any program without the necessary prerequisites but that options are available. Furthermore, community colleges must offer comprehensive programs with alternatives in order to fulfill the promises of access and equity. ◆

Comprehensiveness

The second commitment on which the community college mission rests, and one that relates to open access and equity, is the commitment to comprehensiveness in the college's program offerings. In addition to fulfilling the traditional university parallel function of offering the first two years of the bachelor's program, community colleges offer much more. Although it is impossible and unnecessary for all community colleges to offer all programs, students must have choices in what they study for a community college to accomplish its mission. Without choice in program and course offerings, open access and equity lose much of their meaning. For example, if the college transfer program is the only program offered, the college is not an open-access institution because students have no choice in programs. Many students who come to the community college do not meet the academic requirements for the transfer program; thus, if that program is their only choice, the door to the college is closed to them, and open access is little more than a hollow promise.

To understand why comprehensiveness is so important to the community college, one has only to consider student goals and community needs. By broadening program offerings, community colleges have extended educational opportunities to millions of students ignored by other higher educational institutions. Some students want and need programs that lead quickly to employment. Others have the desire and the opportunity to pursue careers that require lengthier periods of schooling.

> *By broadening program offerings, community colleges have extended educational opportunities to millions of students ignored by other higher educational institutions.*

Community-Based

It is no accident that the word *community* is part of the community college's name. *Community-based* means that a college is committed to serving the needs of a designated geographic area, often called the college's service area or service region. Although the definition of what it means for a community college to serve its community has changed over the years—including an expansion of the definition of service area as a result of computer-based distance learning—to be effective, the community college will see its mission as primarily one of providing education to its local community.

Although the needs are as diverse as the communities served by the colleges, and may change over time, most communities have many needs in common and expect their college to meet those needs. Most communities want programs that permit students to transfer into a bachelor's degree program. Most want vocational and technical training, often including training that meets the specific needs of a local industry. They expect a choice of credit and noncredit courses that lead to certificates, degrees, and diplomas. Most want the college to offer remedial or developmental courses that will assist students to qualify for college-level work. Most communities want courses and activities that meet the recreational, social, and cultural needs of the community. Not every community college can meet all the needs of its service area, but within sometimes serious resource constraints, community colleges strive to meet community needs and maintain standards of excellence. Many ommunity colleges, working closely with local employers, design and offer programs that provide a quick avenue to employment in fields for which there is a well-documented need.

Although cultural and social activities may not be part of the college's formal educational program, such activities enhance education and community life. Most observers agree that it is important for community colleges to sponsor art exhibits, sports events, concerts, drama productions, health fairs, community forums, and other activities that enrich the lives of the people served by the college. The decision to sponsor one event rather than another may be the result of a broad need in the community (a health fair, for example), or may be the result of an individual or group's desire to sponsor an activity. Whatever the reason, it is important that the college respond to the community's professed needs, thereby enhancing the college's educational mission.

Programs and activities overlap, and sometimes there is a fine line between an activity that is part of a formal educational mission or simply a community service. Colleges seek to remain flexible enough to respond to diverse community needs while maintaining integrity as institutions of higher education.

Teaching and Learning

The community college is devoted first and foremost to teaching and learning. Publishing in academic periodicals is not a mandatory aspect of the faculty's role, although this does not preclude community college faculty from publishing or presenting at conferences. Outstanding teachers may be devoted scholars, keeping up with their fields and sharing new developments with colleagues and students. The most important challenge of community college instructors is to develop the ability to adjust styles of teaching to the diverse learning styles of students, and community college faculty and administrators take great pride in their commitment to teaching and learning.

The community college is devoted first and foremost to teaching and learning.

Fostering Lifelong Learning

In the past, people may have assumed that education was an activity a person engaged in for a certain number of years, and when the student graduated, he or she would never return to the classroom. Now, however, more people see learning as a lifelong pursuit. Many find they must continue to engage in formal learning activities, such as those offered at the community college, to keep up with the skills and knowledge required for their jobs, and to be responsible and productive citizens. The U.S. Department of Education reports that enrollment of adults aged 40 or older increased from 17 percent in 1993 to 21 percent in 1997.

The community college's commitment to lifelong learning encompasses an almost limitless number of credit and noncredit courses, activities, and programs designed to enhance the lives of the people in the college's service region for as long as they have the desire to learn. Students, many of whom are older adults, return to the classroom to learn new job skills and improve existing ones. A recent trend is the growing number of students returning to community college after completing a master's or other advanced degree.

The community college's commitment to lifelong learning encompasses an almost limitless number of credit and noncredit courses, activities, and programs designed to enhance the lives of the people in the college's service region for as long as they have the desire to learn.

One of the strengths of the community college is that it makes little distinction between the lifelong learner and the full-time student in terms of the programs and courses in which students may enroll. Many of the courses and programs lifelong learners choose are the same as those designed for degree-seeking students. As older adults return to the community college to upgrade their skills or learn new ones, the distinction between the adult learner and the full-time younger student diminishes.

3 ◆ *Implementing the Mission* _____

*T*he community college achieves its mission through a number of programs, activities, and services. These include college transfer programs, occupational-technical programs, developmental education, community services including employee training, and a variety of support services.

College Transfer Programs

The great majority of the nation's community colleges offer transfer programs through which students can complete the first two years of college. Students enrolled in transfer programs take courses almost identical to those they would take in a bachelor's degree program at a four-year college or university. Most of the courses are in the humanities, mathematics, sciences, and social sciences. The most beneficial transfer programs are coordinated to allow transfer of credits for both general degree requirements and program-level courses.

Community college transfer programs enjoy great success. Some states accept transfer students earning the associate degree into the four-year university system without question. Most students who take the first two years of the four-year degree at a community college are successful in transferring their work to both private and public four-year institutions. U.S. Department of Education studies indicate that the academic records of community college students who transfer tend to compare favorably with those of the students who began their academic careers at four-year institutions.

Occupational-Technical Programs

Occupational-technical education programs have been an important part of the public community college's curriculum since the 1920s, and they remain essential for the United States to compete in a global economy and American workers to keep up with the changing skills needed in the workplace.

In the beginning, most junior colleges limited their occupational programs to teacher training, office

TABLE 3.1

Five Most Frequently Conferred Associate Degrees by Major Field of Study: 1996–97

Degree	# Awarded
Liberal arts, general studies, humanities	167,448
Health professions & related sciences	76,848
Business management & administration services	71,766
Engineering-related technologies	20,208
Protective services	17,445

Source: National Center for Education Statistics

Occupational-technical education programs remain essential for the United States to compete in a global economy.

skills, and the agricultural sciences. Over time, many of these programs evolved into baccalaureate programs and have been replaced at community colleges by programs in fields as diverse as early childhood education, office management, laser optics, medical and computer technologies, auto body repair, and fire science. A series of federal programs—including the Vocational Act of 1963, its 1968 and 1972 amendments, and the Carl D. Perkins Act of 1984 and its later reauthorizations—have strengthened community colleges' capacity to develop new occupational-vocational programs.

TABLE 3.2

Top Five Hot Programs at Community Colleges by Starting Salary: 1997

Program Name	Average Starting Salary
Dental hygiene	$31,750
Manufacturing process technology	$30,675
Telecommunications/interactive information specialists	$29,268
Physical therapy assistant	$28,782
Registered nursing	$28,777

Source: American Association of Community Colleges

TABLE 3.3

Median Earnings for Persons 18 or Older by Highest Level of Educational Attainment: 1996

Highest Degree Attained	Earnings
No high school diploma	$17,148
High school graduate (includes equivalency)	$22,502
Some college, no degree	$26,090
Associate degree	$29,457
Bachelor's degree	$36,525
Master's degree	$45,053
Professional degree	$65,916
Doctorate	$56,758

Source: U.S. Bureau of the Census

Developmental Education

A number of terms are used to describe precollege courses offered at community colleges. Some use *developmental education*, others use *remedial education*, and others refer to these courses as *compensatory education*. Regardless of the name, courses that prepare students to enter college-level courses are an important part of a community college's offerings.

It is not possible to describe the students who require developmental courses in simple terms. Some of the brightest students enrolling in a community college may need precollege courses before enrolling in a degree program. For example, someone who has been out of the job market and without formal schooling for 10 years and who wishes to enroll in a community college nursing program may need precollege courses in mathematics or science. Students who may not have acquired basic skills because of language barriers, a learning disability, or other learning impediments brought on by various life circumstances may need courses in English, writing, or math. In general, it is the community college perspective that society cannot afford to leave anyone behind, and that developmental education is a crucial part of the commitment to access, student success, and community building.

Why Do Community Colleges Offer Remedial Education?

For one reason or another, millions of people in the United States reach adulthood without the education necessary to compete for high-skilled jobs. Poverty, discrimination, and hardships brought on by living in single-parent families are some of the situations that contribute to children and adults' failing to reach their potential for educational attainment and gainful employment. Workers laid off from jobs midway through their career may lack the skills to reenter the ever-changing workforce. Immigrants who lack English-language skills also may struggle to find employment. The number of unskilled jobs is decreasing and the number of high-skilled jobs increasing. If people continue to reach adulthood without the education needed for 21st-century jobs, unemployment among unskilled workers will rise, contributing to poverty and social decline. For the nation to remain strong, the population must be educated to meet the needs of 21st-century employers.

Community colleges have the tools to help respond to this educational crisis. All community colleges offer remedial education—or developmental education—designed to bring students up to a level of competency necessary to participate in college program-level courses or to gain productive employment. Whatever the reason that students have not met the requirements previously, community colleges offer this avenue for them to improve their skills. Although community college students must meet certain prerequisites before they are allowed to progress into academic programs, students who lack the prerequisites still have a place at the community college, with diverse options for learning.

An educated population is vital to the nation's economic and social health. As institutions devoted to universal higher education, community colleges offer remedial education as an important part of fulfilling the community college mission. ◆

Figure 3.1

Employers Who Would Recommend
Community Colleges for Workforce Training

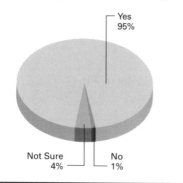

Source: Zeiss, et al. 1997. *Developing the World's Best Workforce.*
Washington, D.C.: Community College Press, American Association
of Community Colleges.

Community Services

Community services, or continuing education, is the most flexible and broad
area of community college offerings. It
includes courses and activities that are
often paid for by participants rather than
by tax dollars. Offerings may range from
hobby courses such as floral arranging or
automobile maintenance to training in
information technology or emergency
medical treatment.

Business and industry look to community colleges to provide on-demand
skills training for workers in their service
area, and contract training is a growing aspect of the community services function at community colleges. The colleges have the flexibility
to respond quickly to the training needs of business and industry, in
part because much of what is taught under the community services
umbrella does not require approval by the governing board or state
coordinating agency. Many community colleges enjoy highly successful relationships with prominent companies in their service area.

Support Services

The community college's open-access admissions policy has ethical
implications as well as educational ones. The college has an ethical
obligation to see that students who enroll have a reasonable chance of
achieving academic success, assuming they do their part. To succeed
academically, students often require a number of support services
beyond classroom instruction. With this in mind, community colleges
maintain learning resource centers containing books, films, videos,
and any number of materials and equipment that enhance learning.

In addition, community colleges provide a network of support
services designed to provide students with assistance as they work
toward their academic goals. This assistance may be available through
writing laboratories, academic advising, personal and career counseling, employment advice, transfer information for those wishing to
pursue a bachelor's degree, career planning, financial aid counseling,
and any number of services that help fulfill the promise of the community college's open door. Open-access admissions can succeed only
if students receive the assistance they need for academic achievement.

4 ◆ *Students and Faculty* _____

*F*or an idea of who attends community college, go to any town or city that has a community college, stand on a street corner, and watch people go by. Take away most people under 18, and most over 50, and the parade that passes will look much like students at a typical community college. Included will be men and women who work full-time and part-time, people from all walks of life and of diverse racial and ethnic backgrounds, unemployed and underemployed individuals, and recent high school graduates.

The ranks of students may include a medical technician wanting to keep up with the latest in the field, a factory worker seeking to upgrade skills, a retired person or homemaker needing to learn or upgrade computer knowledge in order to reenter the workforce, or traditional college students enrolled in the transfer program. The list is as long as the needs, desires, and dreams of people in towns across the nation. The common theme is that the students have discovered the community college and are using it to fulfill their educational needs.

To understand the perspective of today's community college students— and in fact, that of a growing number of four-year students as well—it is helpful to view them from a different perspective than the one through which college students are traditionally viewed. Traditional-age college students, those aged 18 to 21, are customarily perceived as being in a holding pattern, waiting until graduation to assume the rights and responsibilities that accompany full citizenship. Their role is one of student as citizen, with

FIGURE 4.1

First-Time Freshmen in Higher Education: 1997

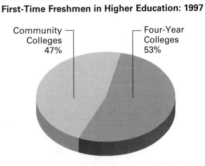

Community Colleges 47%
Four-Year Colleges 53%

Source: National Center for Education Statistics

FIGURE 4.2

Fall Headcount Enrollment in Community Colleges by Age: 1997

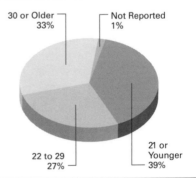

30 or Older 33%
Not Reported 1%
22 to 29 27%
21 or Younger 39%

Source: National Center for Education Statistics

FIGURE 4.3a

Percentage of White and Minority Community College Students: 1997

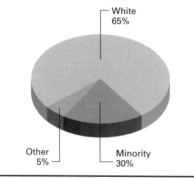

White
65%

Other
5%

Minority
30%

Source: National Center for Education Statistics

FIGURE 4.3b

Percentage Breakdown of Minority Students: 1997

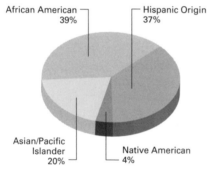

African American
39%

Hispanic Origin
37%

Asian/Pacific Islander
20%

Native American
4%

Source: National Center for Education Statistics

the student role dominant. One result is that the student-citizen is somewhat isolated from the real world of work (even though many such students have part-time jobs), from family responsibilities, and from other rights and responsibilities that will come when they finish college.

Many community college students, especially the more than four million who attend college part time, have reversed the role of student-citizen to one of citizen-student. The citizenship role, rather than the student role, is dominant. The citizen-student is concerned with paying taxes, working full time, supporting a family, paying a mortgage, and other responsibilities associated with the everyday role of a full-time citizen. College attendance is important but often depends upon the availability of money and time.

The citizen-student role has implications for how courses are taught (more emphasis on the students' experiences and knowledge), when they are taught (in the evening and on weekends), and, in some cases, by whom they are taught. As many community colleges have discovered, the citizen-student role requires an entirely different approach to extracurricular activities for most students. The single parent with small children who attends class one night a week is unlikely to attend the Friday night dance at the college. The reporter on the local newspaper is unlikely to serve on the staff of the college newspaper. It is not that the dance or the newspaper or any other activities are unimportant. It is that educating the citizen-student requires a different approach to enhance the college experience.

While recognizing the needs of the citizen-student, the community college cannot neglect those students who attend the community college expecting a more traditional college experience, including extracurricular activities that afford opportunities to develop leader-

Many community college students, especially the more than four million who attend college part time, have reversed the role of student-citizen to one of citizen-student.

ship and social skills. As is true for the students whose citizenship role is dominant, meeting the needs of those students for whom the college experience is dominant requires planning, including academic advising and mentoring by faculty. Because these students are often preparing to transfer to a four-year institution, they may require more attention than the student who is taking one course or noncredit courses.

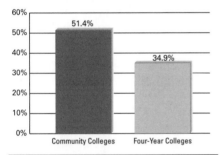

FIGURE 4.4

Percentage of First-Time Students Who Are First-Generation Students: 1995–96

Source: National Center for Education Statistics

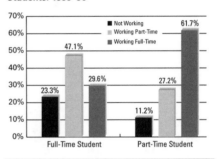

FIGURE 4.5

Employment Status of Community College Students: 1995–96

Source: National Center for Education Statistics

Faculty Dedicated to Teaching and Learning

Faculty, whether full-time or part-time, are the heart of a learning institution. Community colleges employ more than 104,000 full-time faculty and approximately 190,000 part-time faculty. Most full-time faculty at community colleges have a master's degree, and an increasing proportion (16 percent) hold a doctoral degree.

Many community colleges have academic ranks (professor, associate professor, assistant professor, instructor) similar to faculty ranks at four-year institutions. Some community colleges have academic systems based upon longevity, performance, and other factors that determine status and pay. Many community colleges grant academic tenure. Community colleges without a faculty tenure system have some means of reappointing faculty, such as a system of multiyear appointments or a ranking system that ensures job continuity, much like the civil service system. Some community college faculty members belong to labor unions.

An Opportunity to Excel _____

Many people begin their higher education at a community college and continue on to achieve national recognition in a variety of fields. Community colleges are proud of these outstanding alumni, who reinforce the fact that success is often a matter of personal commitment and taking advantage of the opportunities at hand.

One community college alumnus who made particularly valuable contributions to his time was Jackie Robinson, who attended Pasadena City College in California before going on to study at the University of California and then to make history as the first African American to play major league baseball in the 20th century. Robinson not only broke down the color barriers in baseball but frequently spoke out to help further the cause of civil rights.

Household names such as Robinson, Walt Disney, and Calvin Klein are names of community college alumni. Countless more former students have excelled in their chosen fields, even if their achievements are less universally known. K. Kristene Koontz Gugliuzza, M.D., began her studies at Lake Land College, in Illinois, and went on to become one of only a small number of women kidney/pancreas transplant surgeons in the country. M. Anthony Burns, alumnus of Dixie College, Utah, became president and CEO of Ryder System and showed community support and leadership in responding to the devastation of Hurricane Andrew by donating needed resources that Ryder could offer.

Flying seems to be an area to which outstanding alumni gravitate. Mildred "Micky" Axton, alumna of Coffeyville Community College in Kansas, was the first female to fly a B-29 bomber. Astronaut Robert "Hoot" Gibson attended Suffolk County Community College in New York, and Fred Haise, who flew the famed Apollo 13 mission, attended Mississippi Gulf Coast Junior College. Eileen Collins, alumna of Corning Community College in New York, also became a NASA astronaut and in 1999 was named the first female U.S. Space Shuttle Commander.

Community college alumni have proved themselves worthy role models and valuable contributors to society. Meanwhile, each day community college students work toward their goals, whether or not they are widely celebrated. Rising the next step in a career path or learning the skills needed to win employment to support a family can be a personal if not public triumph. There are many paths to success, and those paths frequently and sometimes surprisingly start with a first step through a community college door. ◆

Faculty, whether full-time or part-time, are the heart of a learning institution.

In keeping with the mission, community college faculty members' primary responsibility is teaching. In addition, faculty members reserve an average 9.2 hours per week for office hours and serve as academic advisers to students, helping them plan their programs of study. Faculty members also work with students as sponsors of clubs, community service projects, newspapers, literary publications, and other extracurricular activities.

Many community college faculty members maintain ties to their disciplines through reading and writing, and by attending the meetings of their professional associations. In addition to national organizations, most states have organizations devoted to the advancement of teaching in the community college. Faculty members sometimes volunteer for internships in businesses to ensure that the skills they teach are up-to-date and pertinent to current employment.

A large percentage of community college faculty are part-time. Part-time faculty members teach for a number of reasons. Teaching is a way to fulfill a civic duty, a forum for sharing knowledge with others, and a way of facilitating learning. Most part-time faculty teach only one course per term (3 credit hours), whereas full-time faculty members normally teach five courses (15 credit hours). This scheduling means that most community college courses are taught by full-time faculty members.

Part-time faculty play an important role in assisting the community college to be a comprehensive institution of higher education by bringing specialties to the college that may not be available among full-time faculty. For example, most colleges would not have a full-time faculty member available to teach courses in real estate, whereas qualified instructors are readily available in any community with a viable real estate market. Similarly, a local banker can bring practical experience to the community college classroom that might be unavailable among full-time faculty. Many community colleges can offer certain specialized courses and programs only through the

FIGURE 4.6

Employment Status of Community College Faculty: 1973 to 1997

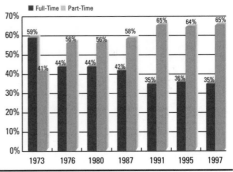

Source: National Center for Education Statistics

*Community college faculty members'
primary responsibility
is teaching.*

use of part-time faculty. For example, it is often necessary for a small college to employ part-time faculty members for courses in art, music, some languages, and technology fields.

As faculty members who joined community colleges during the boom years of the 1960s and 1970s retire, community colleges will recruit new instructors in a highly competitive market. Faculty members will be expected to have a command of technology to the extent needed to teach their courses effectively. Instructors will be more likely to use a variety of teaching methods in addition to lecture, to help facilitate the learning of students who may have diverse ways of assimilating knowledge.

5 ◆ *Funding and Governance* _____

Community colleges receive most of their funding from federal, state, and local taxes, with by far the greatest support coming from state and local tax sources. On average nationally, community colleges receive approximately 39 percent of their funds from state taxes, 18 percent from local government, 20 percent from tuition and fees, 13 percent from the federal government, and 10 percent from other sources.

As is true with so much else about community colleges, funding is characterized by its diversity and varies from state to state and, in some cases, from college to college within a state. While some community colleges receive large portions of their budgets from local sources, others receive little or no local tax support.

Tuition and fees, to a varying degree, provide an important source of income for all community colleges. On average nationally, public community colleges charge about $1,300 for tuition and fees annually. Nevertheless, tuition and fees charged at community colleges vary greatly. Among the states at the high *Funding varies from state to state and, in some cases, from college to college within a state.* end of the tuition scale are Massachusetts, Minnesota, New Hampshire, and New York. Among those at the lower end of the scale are California, North Carolina, and Texas.

Community colleges receive funds from other sources as well. For example, many community colleges offer noncredit courses and activities through their community services and continuing education divisions. These courses are normally paid for by those taking the course or participating in the activity. Sometimes the courses are paid for by businesses who contract with the colleges to train or retrain workers for specific jobs. Contract training is a growing source of revenue for community colleges.

Many community colleges are beginning to supplement their revenues by establishing educational founda-

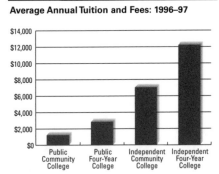

FIGURE 5.1

Average Annual Tuition and Fees: 1996–97

Source: National Center for Education Statistics

tions. Foundations are common for four-year colleges but have been part of the community college picture only recently. These nonprofit organizations are incorporated to receive endowments and other types of funds for use by the community college with which they are affiliated. Some colleges place major emphasis on raising funds from private sources and are very successful in obtaining funds. Other colleges place little emphasis on private fundraising.

In the final analysis, the funding package depends on the social, political, and economic conditions as well as the funding history of a community college in a given state or even a given geographic area within a state. Regardless of funding sources, community colleges have kept student costs relatively low. Community college presidents, the American Association of Community Colleges, and local and state political leaders seek to ensure that tuition and fees remain reasonable. Similarly, national political leaders have helped promote open access through student aid programs.

Regardless of funding sources, community colleges have kept student costs relatively low.

Community College Governance

In the academic world, governance is the process through which institutional decisions are made. The governing process is influenced by rules, regulations, committees, formal and informal groups and leaders, organizational structure, and the history and culture of the institution. All of these components constitute the internal forces that affect a community college and its governance. Individuals and groups outside the institution also affect governance. The most important internal influence on governance is the formal organization, which has the college president at its center. The most important influence on community college governance is the governing board of trustees.

Community colleges have formal organizational structures, just as companies and universities do. The president of the college, as chief executive officer, is responsible for the college's daily operation. In addition, community colleges have vice presidents, deans, department chairs, and others who organize and supervise administrative support for the faculty, staff, and students. Various committees, collegewide forums, college councils representing all segments of the college, and the president's cabinet enhance the governing process. Faculty members participate through service on committees and councils and by voicing their opinions at open forums. Many community colleges involve support staff in the governing process. On some campuses, both the support staff and the faculty belong to labor unions. These unions influence how the college is governed.

The president of the college is responsible to the college's governing board or, in the case of some state systems, to a chancellor, who in turn reports to the governing board. The president is responsible for seeing that the rules and regulations established by the governing board are followed. The president also has the responsibility for keeping the board informed about all aspects of the college's operation, often serving as secretary to the board. Some community college presidents are members of the governing board, often functioning as nonvoting members. The effective president and board work together as a team, each recognizing the other's sphere of authority and responsibility.

The governing board is legally responsible for the community college's well-being. The board makes the policies that the president implements and oversees. Some boards approve budgets, programs, and personnel, and other boards delegate these functions to the president. Normally, effective boards do not *The effective president and board work together as a team, each recognizing the other's sphere of authority and responsibility.* become involved in the daily operation of the college, recognizing that this area is the president's responsibility. Community college governing boards are responsible for the employment, evaluation, and termination of the college president. In choosing the president, the board plays a major role in determining how the college is administered and led.

Elected Boards

Some states have locally elected boards made up of individuals who reside in the college's service area. In many of these states, would-be trustees campaign for board membership, much as they would if they were running for any political office. They are elected for a given term and must seek reelection if they wish to continue to serve on the board. One argument for elected boards is that because they are elected by the people, they are responsive to and responsible to the people who elect them. The counterargument is that because voter turnout is usually small for board elections, those who do vote have an agenda in mind. Therefore, the elected board member may be under the influence of special interests. In any event, elected boards have built strong community college systems, including those in Kansas, Arizona, California, Michigan, and Texas.

Appointed Boards

Some states have locally appointed boards made up of persons who reside in the college's service area. These boards may be appointed by the governor (the most common practice), by other political leaders, or by a combination of the two. Some educators believe the loyalty of appointed board members will be to the appointing official, not to the community college. On the other hand, appointed board members do not spend time and money on an election. Thus, they may have more time for college board work. States with appointed boards include those in Florida, Illinois, North Carolina, and Washington.

State Boards

Still other states are governed by state-level boards. State board members are normally appointed by the governor and serve for specific terms. In contrast to locally appointed and elected boards, state board members are selected from across the state. As a group, they do not reside in any single college's service area.

Critics of state-level boards maintain that they erode local control of the college and that without local control the college will not serve its community as well as it would if its board members were from the college's service area. Some states with state-level boards have local college boards that represent local interests and advise the state board on local matters. As with locally appointed boards, some fear that the loyalty of state board members will be to the governor and not to the local colleges. States with state-level boards include Alabama, Virginia, and the State University of New York system.

6 ◆ A History of Innovation———————————

*A*mong the many innovations of the early 20th century were experiments in higher education, and many people and institutions contributed to a growth spurt in higher education in those years. One of the earliest public junior colleges grew out of the high school in Joliet, Illinois. In 1901, the Joliet Township school board authorized the offering of "postgraduate" education beyond high school coursework. In 1916, the postgraduate division was separated from the high school and, in 1917, was formally renamed Joliet Junior College. As one of the nation's first, and most successful, junior colleges, Joliet was important for several reasons:

- It demonstrated that a well-equipped public high school could offer college-level courses equal to those offered by a university.
- It demonstrated the feasibility and desirability of using tax dollars to offer postsecondary education in the community.
- The needs of the community helped shape the courses and programs offered by this community-based institution.
- The acceptance of courses offered at Joliet by the University of Chicago and Northwestern illustrated the feasibility and practicability of transferring courses from a public junior college to a university.

In 1907, California passed legislation authorizing high schools to offer the first two years of college; in 1917, the state legislature reaffirmed the right of local school districts to organize public junior colleges. In 1921, the legislature authorized the establishment of independent junior college districts governed by local boards. With the passage enabling legislation in California and, in 1917, in both Kansas and Michigan, the growth of public junior colleges, the movement gathered steam. During the first quarter of the 20th century, Texas, Oklahoma, Illinois, Mississippi, Missouri, Iowa, Kansas, and Michigan were among the states that established public junior colleges. Today, every state has one or more public community colleges.

One of the earliest public junior colleges grew out of the high school in Joliet, Illinois.

A National Association

Early in the 20th century, junior colleges felt a need to join together to articulate the role and mission of the two-year college. A group of presidents representing public and independent junior colleges met in St. Louis in 1920 at a meeting called by the U.S. commissioner of education. As a result of this meeting, an organization was conceived that would function as a forum for the nation's two-year colleges. The group became known as the American Association of Junior Colleges (AAJC). In 1930, the first issue of the *The Junior College Journal* was published.

In 1972, the name of the national organization was changed to the American Association of Community and Junior Colleges (AACJC), reflecting the community orientation of most public two-year institutions. In 1992, the name was changed to its current form, the American Association of Community Colleges (AACC).

Today, AACC has more than 1,000 member colleges. The association provides a forum for discussing community college issues and serves as the point of contact for the nation's federal and state agencies, the office of the president of the United States, state governors, international governments, scholars of higher education, the news media, businesses, and others who wish to learn more about community colleges. AACC is the chief advocate and lobbyist for community colleges at the national level.

GI Bill

As World War II was winding down, the nation's policymakers struggled to determine what to do with the millions of servicemen and servicewomen who would soon return to civilian life. Recalling the prewar economic depression, the nation's leaders and citizens feared there would not be enough jobs to absorb those returning from military service.

The nation's political leaders had an answer that would delay the returning military personnel's entry into the job market, improve their skills, and reward them for serving their country: Send them to college. The U.S. Congress passed the Servicemen's Readjustment Act in 1944, a major milestone in federal financing of education. Known as the GI Bill of Rights, this act helped break financial and social barriers for millions of Americans who had served in World War II. The public junior college, along with the rest of higher education, received boosts in enrollment as a result.

The GI Bill, which provided what amounted to a scholarship for every eligible veteran, set a precedent for the student

The GI Bill set a precedent for the student financial aid that exists today.

financial aid that exists today, especially the idea that students should not be barred from college attendance for financial reasons, and that they should have choices in the colleges they attend and the programs they study. The philosophy of the GI Bill and of later student aid programs has had, and continues to have, enormous impact on community college enrollment, in the diversity of students enrolled, and on programs and mission.

Truman Commission Report

Early in 1947, less than two years after the end of World War II, a report of the President's Commission on Higher Education for American Democracy, commonly known as the *Truman Commission Report*, was written to help ensure that higher education would play a major role in preserving and enhancing the democratic ideals for which the nation's citizens had fought during the war. The commission asserted that 49 percent of high school graduates could profit from two years of education beyond high school and sought a way to encourage more opportunity for college attendance.

The commission, chaired by junior college advocate and then-president of the American Council on Education George Zook, believed that an important way to break down the barriers to higher education was to establish a network of publicly supported two-year institutions. The commission introduced the term *community college*.

Community colleges, the commission suggested, should place major emphasis on working with the public schools. They should be within reach of most citizens, charge little or no tuition, serve as cultural centers for the community, offer continuing education for adults as well as technical and general education, be locally controlled, and be a part of their state's and the nation's higher education system.

Growth in the 1960s

After a slow period in the 1950s during which community colleges struggled to find secure footing and a number of independent colleges closed or converted to four-year institutions, the 1960s ushered in an extraordinary era of new growth. Between 1960 and 1970, 457 new colleges opened throughout the country.

Factors that helped fuel the boom of colleges in the 1960s included legislative actions such as the passage of the Higher Education Act, which provided greater federal support to education, and California's Proposition 13, which signaled a trend toward states rather than local entities paying an increasing share of community college costs. Social forces that helped encourage growth in the colleges include a peak in the number of baby boomers coming of age at the time as well as such influences as the end of school segregation in the South, bolstering commitment to access and equity.

Increased Size and Scope

During the second half of the 20th century, community colleges grew more comprehensive in their offerings. They remained committed to providing the first two years of a liberal arts baccalaureate education, but they also responded to economic downturns with commitment to workforce retraining and community development. Local and state governments and the federal government offered varying levels of support, and some colleges thrived more than others.

In 1988, the report *Building Communities: A Vision for a New Century* resulted from a series of meetings sponsored by the W. K. Kellogg Foundation and the Metropolitan Life Foundation and facilitated by the American Association of Community and Junior Colleges Commission on the Future of Community Colleges. The report listed recommended goals for community colleges and introduced the idea that "the word *community* should be defined not only as a region to be served, but also as a climate to be created."

Sponsors and Partners

A number of corporations and educational affiliates have shown long-term support for community colleges. The W. K. Kellogg Foundation and the Ford Foundation, for example, have contributed considerable resources to efforts furthering higher education for all citizens. Grants from corporations such as Microsoft and government entities such as the Department of Labor and the National Science Foundation help fund vital programs in designated AACC focus areas. The American Council on Education and ACT, Inc., are two of the many educational organizations with whom AACC works. Collaboration is the goal and the essential ingredient for bringing about positive changes for colleges, communities, and students.

7 ◆ A New Century _____

At the turn of the 21st century, much has been given to the nation's community colleges, and much is expected from them. Each community college remains uniquely committed, and the colleges continue to find innovative ways to strengthen their educational offerings and remain linked with their communities. Enrolling in a community college will continue to represent for some citizens the best hope of obtaining a college education.

The nation's commitment to lifelong learning is well established. In coming years community colleges can be expected to continue to offer a range of community service courses designed to serve part-time students whose needs are as diverse as society itself.

Community colleges are well positioned to educate much of the nation's workforce, especially in those areas that require less education than a bachelor's degree but more education than a high school diploma. As the nation's economy demands more highly skilled workers in order to compete in world markets, community colleges must continue to excel in workforce development.

New Expeditions: Charting the Second Century of Community Colleges _____

A 1998 grant from the W. K. Kellogg Foundation to the American Association of Community Colleges and the Association of Community College Trustees funded the New Expeditions project to analyze the impact of the 1988 report *Building Communities* and to create a blueprint for community colleges for the 21st century. Drawing upon the knowledge and experiences of community college presidents, trustees, students, professors, educators, and policymakers, New Expeditions examines an array of issues, including governance, funding, open access and equity, technology, faculty roles, leadership development, service to students and communities, and the role of community colleges in improving the quality of civic life. ◆

Faces of the Future Survey_____

AACC and ACT, Inc., have partnered on the groundbreaking study *Faces of the Future*, which will, for the first time, attempt to profile the student body—credit and noncredit—enrolled in American community colleges. Results of the study will provide colleges, legislators, and the public with reliable and focused data describing the diverse clientele who find, in their local community college, the opportunity for growth and enhanced life options. ◆

Some community colleges debate whether to expand their role to offer the bachelor's degree, thus eliminating the need for students to transfer. This debate will continue well into the next century as community colleges constantly redefine what it means to serve their communities. In some cases, this service will include offering the bachelor's degree. However, it is more likely that community colleges will either limit their programs to the associate degree level or enter into agreements with established four-year colleges to offer their programs on the community college campus.

Technology will continue to influence the teaching and learning process at community colleges. Because of the convenience it affords, more students will want to take distance education courses. Competition from for-profit institutions will increase the pressure on community colleges to offer courses at times and places that are convenient for the students. Technology will require an increasingly large percentage of the college's resources, often forcing administrators to choose between personnel and technology.

The expanding use of technology and distance learning have blurred boundaries of college service regions, to include even international sites through computer-based courses. While community colleges will continue to respond to the needs of the immediate geographic area, they will also have to compete with other institutions—private, public, and for-profit—to enroll students.

In the early part of the 21st century, if the economy stays strong, funding from state tax dollars will probably remain stable. Community colleges that wish to expand their programs and services may need to rely on funding sources other than state tax dollars. Institutions may also seek funds from private sources. Federal dollars will continue to be very important to community colleges, especially in the area of student financial aid.

Community colleges serve some 10 million credit and noncredit students per year, and the number is growing. Between 1998–99 and 2007–08, the number of high school graduates is expected to increase by 17 percent, from approximately 2.7 million to 3.1 million. The number of college students, almost 14 million in 1995, will swell to more than 16 million by 2007. This increase in the number of traditional-age college students will challenge all of higher education to respond, and community colleges will be obliged to continue their tradition of innovation in order to maintain their level of service and their commitment to lifelong learning for all adults.

The community college, with its emphasis on serving all segments of society, puts higher education within reach of virtually all who seek it. In the 21st century, the community college's success will continue to depend on its ability to respond to a changing environment. In addition to remaining

In the 21st century, the community college's success will continue to depend on its ability to respond to a changing environment.

flexible and responsive, community colleges must maintain open-access admissions and comprehensive programs to serve an ever-changing population, just as the nation must remain committed to universal higher education.

Milestones in Community College History

1862 *Passage of the Morrill Act*
With its emphasis on agriculture and the mechanical arts, the Morrill Act of 1862, often referred to as the Land Grant Act, expanded access to public higher education, introduced the teaching of new types of courses, and included types of students previously excluded from higher education.

1870 *The Kalamazoo Decision*
The Michigan Supreme Court ruled that local school districts could construct and operate comprehensive high schools from public school funds. This precedent-setting decision opened the way to the development of the modern, comprehensive high school, which would, by the opening of the 20th century, provide many public community colleges with their initial home.

1901 *Founding of Joliet Junior College*
One of the earliest beneficiaries of the construction of large, modern high schools was Joliet Junior College. Founded under the influence of William Rainey Harper, president of the University of Chicago, Joliet Junior College is the oldest continuously existing public two-year college in the nation. While the junior college's courses were initially mixed in with those of the Joliet high school, by 1915 the junior college's enrollment had grown to such an extent that it necessitated the addition of a "junior college wing." This was the nation's first major facility constructed specifically for use by a public junior college.

1904 *The Wisconsin Idea*
The University of Wisconsin emphasized that its mission was to assist the general public through extension services and to provide support to the state government. The university declared that the entire state was its campus. Today,

most community colleges view individual service regions as their campuses.

1917 *Adoption of Junior College Accreditation Standards*
The North Central Association of Schools and Colleges established specific standards for the accreditation of public and private junior colleges. These standards, governing such areas as admissions policies, faculty qualifications, and minimum funding levels, not only brought a degree of uniformity to the young junior college movement but demonstrated the willingness of and capacity for junior colleges to participate in America's unique system of institutional self-regulation.

1918 *Founding of Phi Theta Kappa (PTK) Honor Society*
PTK was founded to recognize and encourage academic achievement by two-year college students and provide them with opportunities for individual growth and development in academics, leadership, and service.

1920 *Founding of the American Association of Junior Colleges*
Called together by Philander Claxton, U.S. commissioner of education, and his higher education specialist, George Zook, more than 25 public and private junior college leaders met in St. Louis to organize the American Association of Junior Colleges. The association, proposed by the U.S. Bureau of Education to function as an accrediting body for the rapidly growing number of junior colleges, became a forum for community college issues and a source of mutual support for its members at a time when the potential of the junior college was not widely understood or appreciated.

1921 *California Legislation Fostering Independent Community College Districts*
Using proceeds from the federal Oil and Mineral Act, the California legislature created a Junior College Fund, the nation's first, to support the operation of locally governed junior college districts operating independently of the public high schools. California's Junior College Act of 1921 came to serve as a model for other states as they sought to put junior colleges on a sound fiscal and policy footing.

1928 *The First State Junior College Board*

Mississippi was the first state in the nation to organize a statewide governing board with specific oversight responsibility for the public junior colleges within its boundaries. The state's governing board worked closely with elected local boards in developing a strong network of public junior colleges that effectively balanced transfer and vocational programs.

1930 *The Asheville Decision*

Even as late as 1930, many state legislatures had yet to adopt specific legislation permitting communities to organize public junior colleges. This legal oversight did not deter communities, which organized junior colleges without explicit legal authority, much as they had organized high schools in the preceding century. The right of a community to take such a step was challenged in Asheville, North Carolina, with the North Carolina Supreme Court eventually ruling in favor of the community and its right to meet the educational needs of its citizens as it best saw fit. This decision did much to secure the legal standing of those public junior colleges that were still being operated without the benefit of state legislation.

1944 *Passage of GI Bill of Rights*

U.S. Congress passed the Servicemen's Readjustment Act, popularly known as the GI Bill, to provide financial assistance for veterans of World War II who wished to pursue higher education. Building on smaller federal student aid programs developed at the end of the Great Depression, the GI Bill represented the federal government's first attempt to provide student aid on a large scale, helping to break down the economic and social barriers to attending college.

1947 *Higher Education for American Democracy*

Published by the President's Commission on Higher Education, this report, popularly known as the *Truman Commission Report*, called for several things, including the establishment of a network of public community colleges that would charge little or no tuition; serve as cultural centers; be comprehensive in their program offerings with an emphasis on civic responsibilities; and serve the area in which they were located. The commission helped popularize the term *community college*.

1958 *Introduction of A.D.N. Programs*

With funding support from the W. K. Kellogg Foundation and Rockefeller family, community colleges in New York, California, Florida, and other states introduced two-year programs leading to an associate degree in nursing that entitled degree holders to sit for licensure as professional nurses.

1960 *W. K. Kellogg Foundation Support of Community College Leadership Development*

The W. K. Kellogg Foundation announced a series of grants to be used to establish university centers preparing a new generation of two-year college leaders. In all, 12 universities established junior college leadership programs. Hundreds of future deans and presidents would eventually graduate from the Kellogg Junior College Leadership Programs.

1960 *California Master Plan for Higher Education*

The three segments of California public higher education—the community colleges, comprehensive colleges and universities, and the University of California—agreed to a voluntary plan to divide responsibility for the state's rapidly growing number of undergraduates and provide the state's residents with the broadest possible range of educational opportunity without wasteful competition among the sectors.

1963– *Federal Aid to Higher Education*
1965

With the adoption of the Higher Education Facilities Act of 1963 and the first Higher Education Act of 1965, the federal government dramatically expanded its direct aid to community colleges and their students. Through the Facilities Act of 1963, communities were given the means to construct new campuses and enlarge existing facilities. Through the Higher Education Act of 1965, and its subsequent reauthorizations, the federal government provided a range of direct grants and loans to students based on need as a means of lessening the barrier of cost to higher education access.

1968 *Creation of the League for Innovation in the Community College*
B. Lamar Johnson founded the League for Innovation to promote experimentation and innovation in community colleges. The League limits its membership to 20 colleges, which are expected to demonstrate outstanding commitment to cutting-edge thinking in leadership and direction of community colleges. Results and information are shared with community colleges across the nation.

1970 *Open Admissions at City University of New York*
Breaking with a long-established tradition of selective admissions, the City University of New York ended its policy of granting admission to only the most academically gifted graduates of New York's public high schools, and guaranteed admission to all high school graduates. This policy change led to a rapid increase in enrollment, the introduction of large-scale developmental programs, and the organization of innovative community colleges in communities with the greatest economic need.

1971– *Federal Aid for Strengthening Tribal Colleges*
1978 Beginning with Navajo Community College in 1971, AACC assisted in winning federal aid for the construction and maintenance of community colleges operating under the jurisdiction of Native American tribes. These efforts culminated in 1978, with the adoption of the Tribally Controlled Community College Assistance Act and the expansion of the community college to previously underserved communities throughout the West.

1972 *Name Change for Association*
The American Association of Junior Colleges changed its name to the American Association of Community and Junior Colleges in 1972 to reflect the broadening terminology used by the institutions.

1972 *Creation of Affiliated Councils*
Councils are organizations whose purposes are consistent with the association's and whose programs contribute to and significantly benefit the association and its members.

Beginning in 1972, councils that meet certain criteria may be eligible for affiliate council membership, which brings with it an added measure of recognition and benefits.

1972 *Establishment of Association of Community College Trustees (ACCT)*
ACCT is the national organization for the nation's community college lay trustees. More than 6,000 trustees govern the nation's community colleges. ACCT places major emphasis on providing trustees with the knowledge, skills, and avenues for influencing public policy at the national and state levels. ACCT works closely with AACC in shaping, achieving, and promoting the community college mission.

1975 *Creation of Presidents Academy*
Composed of chief executives of AACC member colleges, the Presidents Academy provides opportunities for career development through workshops and meetings. Workshops vary in focus but are designed to enhance leadership skills, technology awareness, and public policy awareness in top college officials.

1978 *Proposition 13 in California*
The passage of Proposition 13 in California signaled the beginning of an increased demand by the public for greater accountability from its public institutions. Community colleges have been in the forefront in adopting strategies for ensuring the most effective use of public funds in an era of fiscal constraint.

1988 *Commission on the Future of Community Colleges Report*
The commission's report, *Building Communities: A Vision for a New Century*, defined *community* "not only as a region to be served, but also as a climate to be created." Community colleges were challenged to assume a leadership role in creating a renewed climate of community in their service regions.

1992 *Second Name Change for Association*

The association changed its name to the American Association of Community Colleges in an effort to unify its diverse membership of technical, junior, and community colleges.

1998 *Hope Scholarship and Lifetime Learning Tax Credits Established*

The Hope "scholarship" is a tax credit available to eligible students during their first two years of postsecondary education. The tax credit is available for two tax years to those students who have not completed the first two years of postsecondary education. The Lifetime Learning credit is available for education beyond the first two years of college.

1998 *Workforce Investment Act*

This law substantially alters the federal government's role in job training, adult education, and vocational rehabilitation. Community colleges will still have a major role in the delivery of training services, but there will be a new order in the system. Training will be delivered primarily through Individual Training Accounts (or vouchers) and one-stop career center systems.

1998 *Carl D. Perkins Vocational-Technical Education Act Reauthorization*

The Perkins Act represents the major federal commitment to vocational education activities. The reauthorization removes set-asides historically included in the law for special populations and provides states flexibility in determining how best to spend Perkins dollars. Community colleges are considered important providers of postsecondary vocational education.

Suggested Readings

- Adelman, Clifford. 1992. *The Way We Are: The Community College as American Thermometer*. Washington, D.C.: U.S. Department of Education.

- Baker, George A. III (Ed.). 1994. *A Handbook on the Community College in America*. Westport, Conn.: Greenwood Press.

- Blocker, Clyde E., Robert H. Plummer, and Richard C. Richardson Jr. 1965. *The Two-Year College: A Social Synthesis*. Englewood Cliffs, N.J.: Prentice-Hall.

- Bogue, Jesse P. 1950. *The Community College*. New York: Teachers College Press.

- Brick, Michael. 1963. *The American Association of Junior Colleges*. New York: Teachers College Press.

- Cohen, Arthur M., and Florence B. Brawer. 1996. *The American Community College*. 3d ed. San Francisco: Jossey-Bass.

- Eells, Walter Crosby. 1930. *Bibliography on Junior Colleges, Bulletin, 1930, No. 2*. Washington, D.C.: Government Printing Office.

- Garms, Walter I. 1977. *Financing Community Colleges*. New York: Teachers College Press.

- Gillett-Karam, Rosemary, Suanne D. Roueche, and John E. Roueche. 1991. *Underrepresentation and the Question of Diversity: Women and Minorities in the Community College*. Washington D.C.: Community College Press, American Association of Community Colleges.

- Gleazer, Edmund J., Jr. 1980. *The Community College: Values, Vision, and Vitality*. Washington, D.C.: Community College Press, American Association of Community Colleges.

- Harlacher, Ervin L. 1969. *The Community Dimension of the Community College*. Englewood Cliffs, N.J.: Prentice-Hall.

- Johnson, B. Lamar. 1952. *General Education in Action*. Washington, D.C.: American Council on Education.

- Kalick, Rosanne. 1992. *Community College Libraries: Centers for Lifelong Learning*. Metuchen, N.J.: Scarecrow Press.

• Knoell, Dorothy M. 1966. *Toward Educational Opportunity for All*. Albany, N.Y.: State University of New York.

• McCabe, Robert H., and Philip R. Day Jr., eds. 1998. *Developmental Education: A Twenty-First Century Social Imperative*. San Francisco: League for Innovation in the Community College.

• Medsker, Leland L., and Dale Tillery. 1971. *Breaking the Access Barrier*. New York: McGraw-Hill.

• Roueche, John E., George A. Baker III, and Robert R. Rose. 1989. *Shared Vision: Transformational Leadership in American Community Colleges*. Washington, D.C.: Community College Press, American Association of Community Colleges.

• Roueche, John E., and Suanne D. Roueche. 1999. *High Stakes, High Performance: Making Remedial Education Work*. Washington, D.C.: Community College Press, American Association of Community Colleges.

• Vaughan, George B., and Iris M. Weisman. 1997. *In the Nation's Service: Community College Trustees*. Washington, D.C.: Association of Community College Trustees.

———. 1998. *The Community College Presidency at the Millennium*. Washington, D.C.: Community College Press, American Association of Community Colleges.

• Witt, Allen A., James L.Wattenbarger, Joseph E. Gollattscheck, and James E. Suppinger. 1994. *America's Community Colleges: The First Century*. Washington, D.C.: Community College Press, American Association of Community Colleges.

• Zoglin, Mary Lou. 1976. *Power and Politics in the Community College*. Palm Springs, Calif.: ETC Publications.

Internet Resources

ACT
www.act.org

American Association of Community Colleges
www.aacc.nche.edu

America's Learning eXchange
www.alx.org

Association of Community College Trustees
www.acct.org

Coalition of America's Colleges and Universities—College Is Possible
www.CollegeIsPossible.org

The College Board
www.collegeboard.org

Financial Aid for Students Home Page
www.ed.gov/offices/OSFAP/Students/

National Center for Education Statistics
www.nces.ed.gov

Peterson's
www.petersons.com

U.S. Bureau of the Census
www.census.gov

U.S. Bureau of Labor Statistics
www.bls.gov

U.S. Department of Education
www.ed.gov

U.S. News and World Report–Community Colleges
www.usnews.com/usnews/edu/college/community/commsrch.htm

About the Author

eorge B. Vaughan is a professor of higher education and editor of the *Community College Review* in the Department of Adult and Community College Education at North Carolina State University. Before becoming a professor, Vaughan served as a community college president for 17 years. He is author or coauthor of a number of books and articles on the community college, including *The Community College Presidency at the Millennium* and *Community College Trustees: Leading on Behalf of Their Communities*. He received the 1996 National Leadership Award from the American Association of Community Colleges.